What Is
Lunar New Year?

by Vivian Jun Kirklin

illustrated by Gregory Copeland

Penguin Workshop

For Taylor, Alex, and Bennett,
for the inspiration and encouragement—VJK

To Yuen—GC

PENGUIN WORKSHOP
An imprint of Penguin Random House LLC
1745 Broadway, New York, New York 10019

First published in the United States of America by Penguin Workshop,
an imprint of Penguin Random House LLC, 2025

Visit us online at penguinrandomhouse.com.

Special thanks to our expert reader who provided feedback on the text and illustrations,
Hawthorne Jiahong Sun.

Library of Congress Cataloging-in-Publication Data is available.

Printed in the United States of America

ISBN 9780593888117 (paperback)   10 9 8 7 6 5 4 3 2 1 CJKW
ISBN 9780593888124 (library binding)   10 9 8 7 6 5 4 3 2 1 CJKW

The authorized representative in the EU for product safety and compliance is
Penguin Random House Ireland, Morrison Chambers, 32 Nassau Street,
Dublin D02 YH68, Ireland, https://eu-contact.penguin.ie.

Contents

H. K. Wong

What Is Lunar New Year?

In the 1950s, a man named H. K. Wong lived in California and dreamed of sharing his Chinese culture with his community. Born in San Francisco's Chinatown neighborhood, H. K. was now a respected business leader there. He had always been proud of his heritage and felt lucky to experience it through language, art, and food every day.

As time went on, H. K. began to wonder how he could share his roots with the rest of the community. One day, an idea came to him. What if Chinatown's annual Lunar New Year festival could be a grand celebration for the whole city?

H. K. got to work. Together with the Chinese Chamber of Commerce, he set his sights on

Lunar New Year—which would take place on February 15, 1953. He recruited a huge team of volunteers, and they all worked tirelessly to build a stage, set up sound and lighting, and rehearse performances. The festival would include art exhibits, music and dance shows, the annual Miss Chinatown contest, and a spectacular parade. H. K. and the other planners spread the news widely, hoping to draw a large crowd.

On the day before Lunar New Year, the preparations for the festival were ready. H. K.'s dream was about to come to life. Streets had been transformed into an outdoor museum so visitors could enjoy looking at traditional Chinese art. Children practiced marching with their instruments, getting ready for their big performances. The sharp pop of firecrackers began to echo through the streets.

The next day, Lunar New Year officially arrived!

The festival kicked off in the afternoon with drummers. All afternoon, the stage showcased Chinese orchestras, dancers, and singers.

After sunset, the long-awaited parade got

underway. The grand marshal was Corporal Joe Wong, a Chinese American military veteran. As cars carrying local leaders rolled down the avenue, firecrackers went off at every intersection. Through the smoke, viewers could see floats and lion dancers passing by.

The crowds that packed the streets cheered as a

marching band from a Chinese school paraded by. Next came the newly crowned Miss Chinatown, Pat Kan. She glided through the avenue as she waved and smiled at the crowd.

The climax of the parade was the dragon dance. The dragon was like a long, slithering puppet that took a whole team of people to operate.

The festival continued to light up the night with sword dancers, martial arts demonstrations, a fashion show, juggling, and acrobats. Then the streets opened up for a public dance party, and people in the crowd joined in on the fun.

The next day, newspapers reported on the enormous success of the parade. About one hundred thousand people had attended! One newspaper called it "one of Grant Avenue's greatest days."

Eventually, the festival was expanded and was even broadcast on national television. Today, the Chinese New Year Parade and Festival in San Francisco is the biggest parade celebrating Lunar New Year outside of China. But it's just one example of festivities for a holiday that's celebrated by over a billion people worldwide.

CHAPTER 1
The Origins of Lunar New Year

You may be familiar with New Year's Day, which always occurs on January 1. But did you know that the day of the Lunar New Year changes from year to year? Lunar New Year is New Year's Day on the lunar calendar—a different kind of calendar from the one we typically use. The lunar calendar tells time through the moon's different phases.

Most countries celebrate Lunar New Year between January 21 and February 20. The reason why the date changes is that the lunar calendar doesn't exactly match up with the solar calendar, which is the calendar that countries such as the United States, Canada, Mexico, the United Kingdom, Italy, France, and other Western countries use.

Historians believe the first lunar calendar was developed in Sumer between 4100 and 1750 BCE. Sumer, in what is now southern Iraq, was the first civilization in the world. The Chinese lunar-solar calendar, which sets the day most people around the world celebrate Lunar New Year, dates to about the fifteenth century BCE—which is about three thousand years ago. Back then, farmers needed a way to know when to plant, grow, and harvest their crops. They noticed that it took about twenty-nine and a half days for the moon to go from a new moon (meaning not visible at all) to a full moon and back to a new moon again. That is what a lunar month is. It then took twelve of these lunar months to make up a year of farming seasons.

The calendar we use today is a solar calendar, not a lunar calendar. That means the length of our year matches the time it takes for Earth to orbit around the sun. This is why the timing of lunar months is different from the months of the solar calendar. In addition, the solar year is slightly longer than the lunar year—it is 365 days, while a lunar year is just 354 days.

The Chinese lunar-solar calendar eventually spread to other parts of Asia, where people modified it and used it to mark important days and seasons.

Historians aren't sure exactly when Lunar New Year began to be celebrated, but they believe that the first celebration was in China around 1600 to 1046 BCE, during the Shang dynasty. A dynasty (say: DY-nuh-stee) is a series of rulers (similar to kings and queens) from the same family. From about 1600 BCE to 1912 CE—just over one hundred years ago—China was ruled by dynasties.

King Tang of the Shang dynasty

Lunar New Year is the first day of the first lunar month of the year. This is the day of the first new moon. Since a majority of people in ancient China were farmers, the end of the year was an anxious time. It was the middle of a long, cold period, and rent money was due to the landlords who owned the land that the farmers grew their crops on. Marking the new year was a way of celebrating the coming of spring and the payment of debts to the landlords. A debt is an amount of money that is owed.

During the Han dynasty (206 BCE–220 CE), the time period when the Han family was in power, Lunar New Year traditions became more official. On the first day of the new year,

officials from around the Chinese empire would visit the imperial palace. They brought gifts and bowed before the emperor to show their loyalty. In return, the emperor would give them gifts. The day ended with feasting, music, and a dazzling display in front of the palace. The entertainment included acrobats, dancers, and a huge figure of a beast called Han-li that transformed from a fish into a dragon.

Imperial palace

Historians know less about what ordinary people did to celebrate back then. But what they do know is that Lunar New Year was a family event. From the beginning, it was about being surrounded by loved ones and remembering those who had come before you. The day may have started with the family making sacrifices to their ancestors, probably by offering them food and drink. In the evening, the family might have visited extended relatives and important members of their community.

Lunar New Year customs in China started for many reasons. They helped people get through a long winter and honor their ancestors and elders. But a major reason why they continued for years to come is that Lunar New Year was joyful! The feasting, bright lights, music, and dance of the earliest Lunar New Year celebrations would go on to become beloved traditions.

The Story of Nian

Legends and myths provide more clues about how Lunar New Year traditions came about. One popular legend is the story of Nian (say: nee-ehn). Nian was a terrifying mythical beast whose name also means "year." According to the myth, Nian appeared at the end of winter and threatened to devour villagers and their livestock. One year, a white-bearded man appeared at a village and put on red clothes, placed red paper on doors and windows, and started a bright, crackling fire. Nian was frightened off by this display, and the man, who was actually a god in disguise, rode away on its back. This legend influenced people to decorate with red, light firecrackers and torches, and make loud noises during Lunar New Year.

CHAPTER 2
The Chinese Zodiac

Scholars think that the Chinese zodiac originated more than two thousand years ago. Before the Han dynasty (206 BCE–220 CE), people in China counted years in a number of different ways. It was during the Han dynasty that the system became more standardized. The years were organized into groups of twelve that repeated to create a twelve-year cycle. The Western zodiac is based on constellations in the night sky, which change about every thirty days. The Chinese zodiac, however, is a way of knowing what year it is. If someone asked, "What year is it?" and it was the tenth year in the twelve-year cycle, you could answer, "The year of the rooster!" This is because each year

in the Chinese zodiac has its own animal. There
are twelve animals, one for each year of the cycle.

The animals of the Chinese zodiac have
their roots in folklore and in Taoism. Taoism
is a religion and way of thinking that was
founded in China during the sixth century
BCE. *Tao* means that people and animals
should live in harmony with the universe.

The Jade Emperor

The Jade Emperor, or the ruler of Heaven, is considered one of the most important gods in the Taoist tradition. A popular legend that is often retold today says that the animals of the Chinese zodiac were selected through a race held by the Jade Emperor.

The zodiac has played a role in Chinese culture throughout its history. In the past, people might have used the zodiac to predict how the year's harvest might turn out or to help make big life decisions. In 1912, China officially began to use the Western, or Gregorian, calendar. However, the zodiac is still symbolically important today, especially during Lunar New Year. The arrival of Lunar New Year brings excitement for the new zodiac year. It's thought that your zodiac sign, or the animal assigned to the year you were born, can influence everything from your personality to what kind of career you'll have. When your zodiac animal cycles back around, it might be a particularly lucky year for you!

The Race for the Zodiac

The Jade Emperor, while sitting in Heaven, wanted to make the years easier to remember. He decided to name each year in the twelve-year cycle after an animal. With so many animals to choose from, however, he needed a way to pick only twelve. He decided to hold a race. The twelve animals to cross the finish line first would claim a spot in the zodiac. One of the animals, the rat, was especially

devious. It betrayed its friend the cat by not waking it up before the race. This explains why the cat and the rat are enemies today! The ox would have won first place, but the rat tricked the ox into giving it a ride on the ox's back. So the rat came in first, and the ox came in second, followed by the other ten animals that now make up the Chinese zodiac: the tiger, the rabbit, the dragon, the snake, the horse, the sheep, the monkey, the rooster, the dog, and the pig.

The Chinese Zodiac Animals

Each animal in the Chinese zodiac has a different personality. If you were born in the year of the rooster, perhaps you might be a proud and confident person who loves adventure. If your zodiac animal is the sheep, there's a chance you are a calm and creative person who brings a sense of caring to those around you. Find your birth year and see if your zodiac animal matches your personality!

 Rat (2008, 2020): charming, creative, ambitious, talkative

 Ox (2009, 2021): dependable, loyal, honest, logical

 Tiger (2010, 2022): brave, impulsive, warm, commanding

 Rabbit (2011, 2023): independent, humble, introverted, calm

 Dragon (2012, 2024): extroverted, strong, imaginative, decisive

 Snake (2001, 2013): calm, elegant, intelligent, devious

 Horse (2002, 2014): cheerful, talkative, independent, competitive

 Sheep (2003, 2015): caring, selfless, artistic, trusting

 Monkey (2004, 2016): curious, mischievous, funny, adaptable

 Rooster (2005, 2017): proud, confident, affectionate, adventurous

 Dog (2006, 2018): loyal, honest, trusted, active

 Pig (2007, 2019): forgiving, jolly, hardworking, peaceful

CHAPTER 3
Chūn Jié in Modern China

Lunar New Year celebrations in China have gradually expanded to fifteen days, starting with the first new moon of the year and ending with the first full moon. The first new moon of the year is the start of the lunar year, and it's also considered the beginning of spring. Today in China, Lunar New Year is the biggest holiday of the year and is known as Chūn Jié (say: CHOON-jyeah), which means "Spring Festival." It is an official public holiday, and most people have a week off from work to celebrate it. Children's winter vacations start in late January and go to the middle of February so that they can enjoy the entire festival.

Preparations for Chūn Jié begin many days

before the holiday itself. Stores are crowded
with people shopping for food, gifts, and
decorations. Millions of people pack the roads
and trains as they return to their hometowns
to be with their families. People buy new

clothes and shoes and get their hair cut before Chūn Jié to start the coming year off fresh. Cutting hair during the first lunar month is considered bad luck because some believe it could cut good luck short. Before Chūn Jié, houses are cleaned from top to bottom as a symbol for sweeping away any bad luck from the year before. During Chūn Jié, it is considered bad luck to clean because doing so could sweep away good luck.

Once houses are clean, they are decorated. Flowers and fruits are popular decorations. This is because they represent abundance, long life, and good health. Red-and-gold paper is used in many Chūn Jié decorations because the colors are connected to luck and wealth. One common activity is using red-and-gold paper to write short poems, or couplets, with happy and positive messages. The poems are then hung on doorways to bring in good luck and to welcome visitors.

Lunar New Year's Eve is a time that is all about family. Traditionally, the family gathers together for a big feast. The foods that are served at this

Jiaozi

family feast usually have special meanings. For example, dumplings, or jiaozi (say: JOW-tse), are often served because their shape is like a money bag or gold nugget, and therefore, eating them may attract wealth in the new year. Noodles, shaped like long threads, symbolize a long life. Some foods are eaten because their names simply sound lucky. For example, the word for "orange," *ju*, sounds similar to the word *ji*, which means "good fortune," so celebrators eat oranges.

After the feast, many people choose to change into new clothes to welcome in the new year. It is tradition to wear red garments, so many choose red outfits. People often tell each other "Guo Nian Hao," which means "to pass the year." Finally, at the stroke of midnight, firecrackers are set off! The lights and noise symbolize the scaring away of Nian. Then, the red paper from the used firecrackers is left on the ground because it represents good luck.

The next morning—which is the first day of the new year—is focused on honoring ancestors and elders. The family may light incense sticks that release a fragrant smoke when burned as a tribute to their ancestors. Younger members of the family bow to the elders in the family, such as parents and grandparents, and often offer them tea. In return, the elders give the younger members red envelopes called hongbao (say: hong-bow) that are filled with money. Many people then eat a vegetarian breakfast, such as dumplings filled with vegetables. Vegetables are thought to clean the body and are a good way to start the year fresh.

Hongbao

After honoring elders and ancestors in the home, the family might go out to visit extended relatives, especially the most senior family members. They may also visit neighbors and friends to wish them a happy new year and exchange presents.

The days after Lunar New Year are filled with more get-togethers with family and friends, special meals, and perhaps visits to temples to honor the gods. On the eighth day, many people return to work. Then, as the end of Chūn Jié approaches, preparations for the Lantern Festival get underway.

Lucky Numbers

Colors are very important to Chūn Jié celebrations in China, with red and gold being considered the most lucky. But did you know that certain numbers are considered lucky during Chūn Jié as well? For example, the number eight (*bā*) sounds like the word for "to become wealthy" (*fā*), so it is considered very lucky. The number six (*liu*) is also considered lucky because it is associated with the Chinese word for "flow," so it could predict a smooth and trouble-free life.

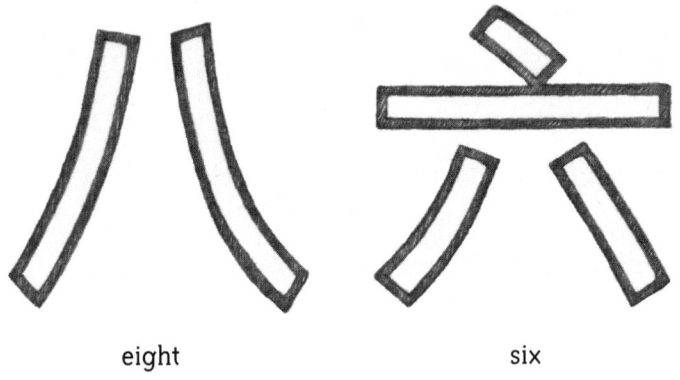

eight   six

On the other hand, the Chinese word for the number four (*si*) sounds very similar to the word for "die" (*sĭ*), so it is considered very unlucky. When filling hongbao with money for children, elders take the meanings of these numbers into account. They typically choose amounts that add up to an eight or a six and avoid unlucky numbers like four.

The Lantern Festival is on the final day of the Spring Festival, the fifteenth day of the year. It is the day of the first full moon. This festival is one of the most spectacular events of the entire Lunar New Year celebration. For days, people prepare by hanging lanterns up all over the streets and buildings. These lanterns symbolize life and hope and are thought to help

Tang yuan

lost spirits return home. Families may also prepare tang yuan, glutinous rice balls that usually have a sweet filling. They are traditionally eaten during the Lantern Festival because they look similar to a round moon.

After the sun sets, parades take place in the glow of the full moon. Children carry lit paper lanterns in all shapes and sizes down the street. The lanterns may be in traditional shapes, such

as circles or rectangles, or they might be shaped like fun objects, such as butterflies, birds, or flowers. Lion and dragon dancers parade down the street to the loud, rhythmic beating of drums and gongs. The parades then cap off with a stunning display of fireworks! This joyous festival is the conclusion to fifteen days of remembering and honoring ancestors, feasting on delicious and meaningful foods, and, most importantly, connecting with family and loved ones.

CHAPTER 4
Seollal

China is just one country that celebrates Lunar New Year, but there are many more places that also celebrate the holiday. Lunar New Year has been celebrated in Korea as far back as 700 BCE, according to historical records. Later, in the years between 935 CE and 1392 CE, known as the Goryeo period, nine major festivals were celebrated throughout the year, and Lunar New Year was one of them. Today, Lunar New Year is called Seollal (say: suh-lol) in Korea, and it is considered the most important traditional holiday of the year.

Like in China, Seollal in Korea is a time for remembering and honoring ancestors and elders. The holiday lasts for three days, including the day before the Lunar New Year, the day of, and the day after. Many people travel in order to be with their extended families.

The morning of Lunar New Year might begin with the family honoring their ancestors by offering them food and tea on a special table.

Children and adults alike then pay respect to
the elder members of the family by bowing in
a tradition called saebae. While bowing, it is
customary to say, "Saehae bok mani badeuseyo,"
which means "Many blessings for the new
year." The elders, whether they are parents,
grandparents, aunts, or uncles, then give the
younger family members money. The money
may be stored in a colorful silk pouch called a
bokjumeoni (say: bok-ju-muh-nee).

During Seollal, many people in Korea wear traditional clothing, known as hanbok (say: hahn-bok). Some people get brand-new hanbok made for Seollal to match the newness of the year. A new set of hanbok especially for Seollal is known as seolbim (say: sul-beem). A hanbok consists of a wrap-style jacket or tunic with long, full sleeves that is fastened in the front with a tie. Under the jacket is either a full skirt or loose-fitting pants. The hanbok that children wear are often the most colorful, and a baby's first time wearing a hanbok is a time for excitement. But for people of all ages, hanbok are a form of cultural celebration and self-expression. Numerous accessories, both traditional and modern, can be added to them, such as hats, slippers, silken tassels, and hair pins. Hanbok come in every color imaginable and are often beautifully embroidered and patterned, making for a vibrant display at Seollal.

Hanbok

The traditional foods of Seollal include dumplings, which are called mandu in Korea; sweet tteok, which are chewy rice cakes in various

Tteokguk

shapes and flavors; and tteokguk, which is a brothy soup filled with white oval-shaped rice cakes that is usually topped with sliced egg and shreds of dried seaweed. Sometimes tteokguk will even have mandu in it. Tteokguk is thought to bring luck and prosperity for the new year since the oval rice cakes resemble coins. According to Korean tradition, you become a year older once you've eaten your tteokguk!

Games and activities are an important part of Seollal. One popular traditional game involves playing on a Korean seesaw. The seesaw is made out of a long wooden board that is propped up in the middle by a bag of straw. But on this seesaw, the two players do not sit on the ends— they stand! To make the seesaw move, each player must jump on their end, sending the player on the other side flying into the air. The game continues with the players taking turns jumping and landing. The player who keeps their balance the longest wins the game.

Another popular outdoor activity at Seollal is flying kites. Kites are traditionally rectangular in shape and are made from sticks and paper. They often feature bold designs in red, blue, yellow, and green. Flying these colorful kites high in the sky is thought to ward off bad luck.

Measuring Age in Korea

The traditional way to measure age in Korea says that babies are automatically one year old when they are born and then become a year older at every new year. In fact, there used to be multiple ways of measuring age in Korea. Another method said babies are zero at birth and then become a year older every January 1. In most official contexts, age was set by the international aging system, which is the one used most commonly around the world. This system says babies are zero when born and turn a year older every birthday.

Having all these systems for measuring age often led to confusion and the need for people to explain their age when traveling outside the country. So in 2023, lawmakers in South Korea officially switched over to the international aging system. People who had measured their age by the traditional aging system then became one to two years younger overnight! If you were born right before the new year, for example, you would have been one year old at birth and then turned two at the new year. But according to the international system, you were zero at birth and didn't turn one until your first birthday, so your age would have rolled back two years.

A favorite indoor Seollal game is yutnori. This game is traditionally played with four sticks that are flat on one side and rounded on the other.

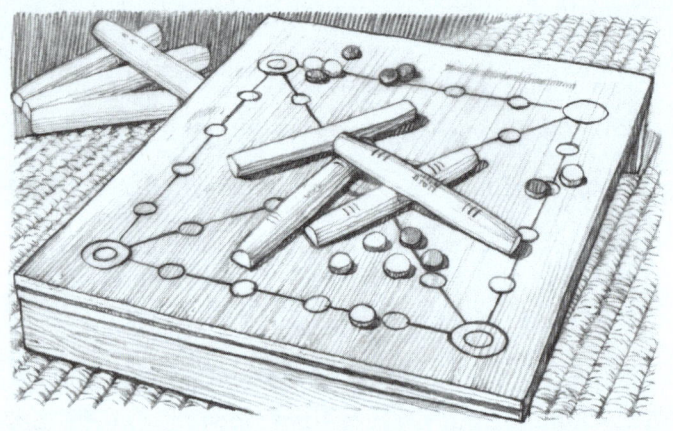

The rounded sides usually have pictures carved or painted onto them. There is also a board made of cloth or paper that has dots around the edges and an X shape through the middle. Players each have a token that they place at the starting position on the board. They take turns tossing the sticks, or yut, into the air. Depending on how the sticks land, a player will move their piece a certain number of spaces along the board. The first person or team to make it back to the start position wins.

Like other Lunar New Year celebrations, the Korean holiday of Seollal is focused on honoring the past while keeping cultural traditions alive in the present. The same threads that run through all of these celebrations—spending time with family, eating festive foods, playing, and having fun—are expressed in a uniquely Korean way during Seollal.

CHAPTER 5
Tet

Lunar New Year in Vietnam is called Tet. The name Tet is short for Tết Nguyên Đán (say: tet nuen dan), meaning "feast of the first morning." As in China and Korea, Lunar New Year is the most important holiday of the year in Vietnam. The festival starts at the end of the old year and can last for up to a week.

In Vietnam, Lunar New Year is a time for emphasizing connections. First, people connect with family. They travel to spend time with their families and try to set aside any disagreements and conflicts, because actions during Tet are thought to set the tone for the entire upcoming year.

On the first day of the new year, the younger family members show their respect for their elders by crossing their arms across their chests and bowing. They are given money in red envelopes in return.

People also connect with family members who have passed away. They may visit the graves of family members in the days leading up to Tet to pay their respects and take care of the grave sites.

On the eve of the new year, many families perform a ritual to invite the spirits of their ancestors to join them for the first three days of the new lunar year. They burn incense, offer food, and say a welcome to the ancestral spirits.

Lunar New Year in Vietnam is a time for remembering people's connection to nature as well. The new year is a good time for recognizing how people are tied to the land and all of life. Natural elements are a key part of Tet celebrations. For weeks leading up to Tet, huge flower markets are set up. Branches of bright yellow apricot blossoms and soft pink peach blossoms are common decorations. Miniature kumquat bushes are popular as well. They usually stand in ceramic pots and have branches full of dark green leaves and ripe golden fruit. These flowers and trees are chosen because they symbolize hope, luck, and longevity.

Another Tet tradition involving plants is the Tet tree, or cay neu (say: kai new). The Tet tree is actually a bamboo pole with its leaves removed except at the top. The cay neu is decorated with objects like tinkling bells, colorful flags, and paper lanterns. Its purpose is to ward off evil demons and bring good luck. A family might place a cay neu in front of their house, or a town might display one in a public square.

Cay neu

A person's connections to their larger community are also an important part of Tet. The first two days of the new year are usually reserved for members of the family, but on the third day, people visit teachers they wish to thank and honor. Some people think that the first outside visitor to the home will affect the luck of the year to come, so the first guest invited to the house at the new year is often an honored or successful family member.

Traditionally during Tet, all cleaning and food preparation is done before the holiday. One of the most essential Tet dishes, banh chung, can stay fresh for days or even weeks, so it is perfect for making or buying in advance. Banh chung is a square cake that is about five to seven

Banh chung

inches long on each side. The cake is made of sticky white rice, filled with layers of savory shredded pork belly and mung beans, wrapped tightly in banana leaves, and then boiled in water for hours. When it's time to eat, the cake is unwrapped and sliced, sometimes fried in a pan, and then served with pickled carrots and daikon radish.

Banh chung is such an important food during

Tet that there is even a legend told about how it was first made. According to the story, a king was planning to step down and needed to pick an heir from his many sons. He told them to go out and find the best dishes in the world. His heir would be the one who brought back his favorite. One of the sons, Lang Lieu, didn't know what to do. But one night, in a dream, a spirit described to him how to make banh chung. He presented it to his father and won the contest, becoming the heir to the throne.

Another important traditional Tet food is mut. Mut is not one thing, but a variety of candied fruits and vegetables, nuts, and seeds presented on a circular tray particularly for guests. Since visits to friends and community members are such an important part of Tet, most families have a supply of mut on hand as snacks. Popular items for a mut tray include candied ginger, candied coconut ribbons, lotus seeds,

Mut

and watermelon seeds. The items might be store-
bought or made at home, but they are always
colorful and eye-catching in addition to being
delicious. As friends and family talk and laugh
around the mut tray, the sweetness of the treats
represents the hope for a sweet year ahead.

The Vietnamese Zodiac

The arrival of Tet brings a new zodiac year. The Vietnamese zodiac is similar to the Chinese zodiac except that two of the animals are different. Instead of the ox, the Vietnamese zodiac has the water buffalo, and instead of the rabbit, there is the cat. Though there is no official explanation for the differences, the use of the water buffalo seems easy to understand because it is considered a

Water buffalo

symbol of Vietnam. Water buffalo were very important farm animals in Vietnam's history and have traditionally been used to plow rice fields. They continue to be used for farm work in some areas. On the other hand, the reason there is a cat instead of a rabbit in the Vietnamese zodiac is more of a mystery. One theory says cats are more popular animals than rabbits in Vietnam because they hunted the rats in rice fields. Another theory says that an older Chinese word for "rabbit," *mao*,

Cat

sounds like the Vietnamese word for "cat," *meo*, so the Chinese zodiac was interpreted differently in Vietnam.

CHAPTER 6
Lunar New Year in the Philippines

The Philippines and China have been trading partners for over a thousand years, and many Chinese people immigrated to the Philippines over that time as well. Through that long history of trade and immigration, China's Lunar New Year traditions became common in the Philippines. Today, celebrating Lunar New Year is more popular than ever there.

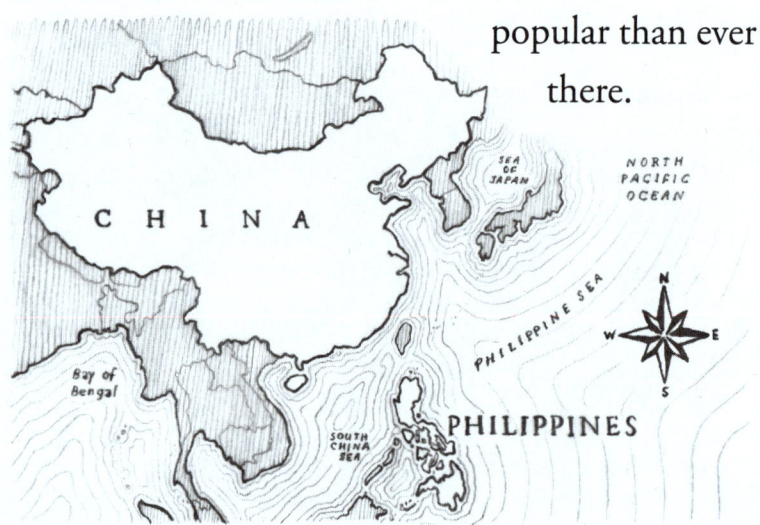

The Filipino New Year's holiday on December 31 shares many similarities with China's Lunar New Year. Before the holiday arrives, people clean their houses, go shopping, and prepare food. They make plans to travel and see their families. On December 31, families get together for a big midnight feast called Media Noche (say: MEH-dee-uh NO-chay), which literally means "midnight." At the stroke of midnight, families light firecrackers, make loud noises to scare away bad spirits, and open windows and doors to welcome in good luck.

Jumping High and Wearing Polka Dots

Though some Filipino New Year's traditions, such as setting off firecrackers and making loud noises, may sound familiar, there are others that are uniquely Filipino. For example, at midnight on December 31, children are encouraged to jump as high as they can into the air. Jumping up and down at the new year is thought to help them grow taller!

Round shapes are considered lucky for the new year in the Philippines. One common tradition for either December 31 or Lunar New Year is preparing a platter of twelve round fruits, such as oranges, melons, and grapes. The roundness of the fruits represents good fortune and prosperity. People may also scatter coins throughout the house to attract wealth for the new year. In fact, roundness is considered so lucky that people will wear polka-dot clothing during their New Year's celebrations! It's not uncommon for whole families to be decked out in brand-new polka-dot dresses, shirts, and pants.

Binondo

In addition to the New Year's holiday on December 31, Lunar New Year was declared an official national holiday in the Philippines in 2015. One major location for Lunar New Year festivities is Binondo, a district in the capital city of Manila. Binondo is known as the world's oldest Chinatown. Each year hundreds of thousands of people gather there for a Lunar New Year festival.

This celebration includes dragon and lion dancers, a parade with floats, and a fireworks show. Other smaller festivals can be found during the week of Lunar New Year as well.

Lunar New Year in the Philippines is centered on family, just like it is in other countries. It is a time for people of all generations to gather together, with grandparents, parents, children, aunts, and uncles all meeting to celebrate. Special visits may be made to elderly members of the family as well.

During Lunar New Year, children and unmarried young adults without jobs (such as college students) receive money from their elders in red envelopes, called ang pao (say: ong pow).

Ang pao

There are traditional rules to follow when getting ang pao. The receiver should of course say many thanks to the giver. Then, the envelopes should not be opened right away. In fact, to be as polite as possible, the receiver shouldn't even look at the envelope but rather put it away in their pocket and count the money later in private. Having money in your pocket during the new year is considered very lucky. Also, the money should be saved rather than spent right away. Saving the money starts the year off in a careful and responsible way. The tradition of ang pao has become so popular in the Philippines that people also give them out on January 1 and other significant days, like birthdays.

Popular foods during Lunar New Year in the Philippines include dumplings, fish, pancit, lumpia, and tikoy.

Pancit

Pancit (say: pan-SEET), which translates to "noodles," is a stir-fried noodle dish with vegetables and meat in a salty-sweet sauce. It is usually made with thin rice noodles, and the vegetables might include carrots, cabbage, and onions. The meat could be chicken, beef, pork, or seafood. Pancit is served with very long noodles to symbolize a long life.

Lumpia are a type of Filipino spring roll. The outside is a paper-thin wrapper that's made of flour and water. The wrappers are filled with meat and vegetables and rolled up into short cylinders. The lumpia

Lumpia

are usually deep-fried until they are very crispy. The golden color of fried lumpia represents good fortune.

Tikoy, also known as nian gao in China, is one of the most symbolic and important foods during Filipino Lunar New Year celebrations. Tikoy is made of sticky rice flour, sugar, and water. The ingredients are mixed together, then steamed in a pan until they form a solid

Tikoy

cake. After the cake is cooled for hours in the refrigerator, it is cut into thin slices and dipped in egg. Then the slices are fried in a pan. The result is a sweet, sticky, and crispy golden-brown cake. The stickiness of the cake symbolizes strong family relationships, or the family "sticking" together.

Eating tikoy and observing other Filipino Lunar New Year customs remind people to appreciate good things like family, health, and financial stability. The new year is an opportunity

to savor the sweetness of making it through
another year filled with joys and challenges with
your family by your side.

CHAPTER 7
Songkran

The traditional new year's celebration in Thailand is called Songkran. This holiday started out being based on the lunar calendar but shifted over time. Now, it is always from April 13 through April 15 on the solar calendar. While most countries that celebrate Lunar New Year do so in late January to early February, the Thai new year was influenced by a combination of both lunar and solar dates, which is why it takes place in a different month.

The great majority of people in Thailand practice the religion of Buddhism, and specifically Theravada Buddhism. Buddhism is a religion that started around the fifth century BCE in India, and Theravada Buddhism is considered one of

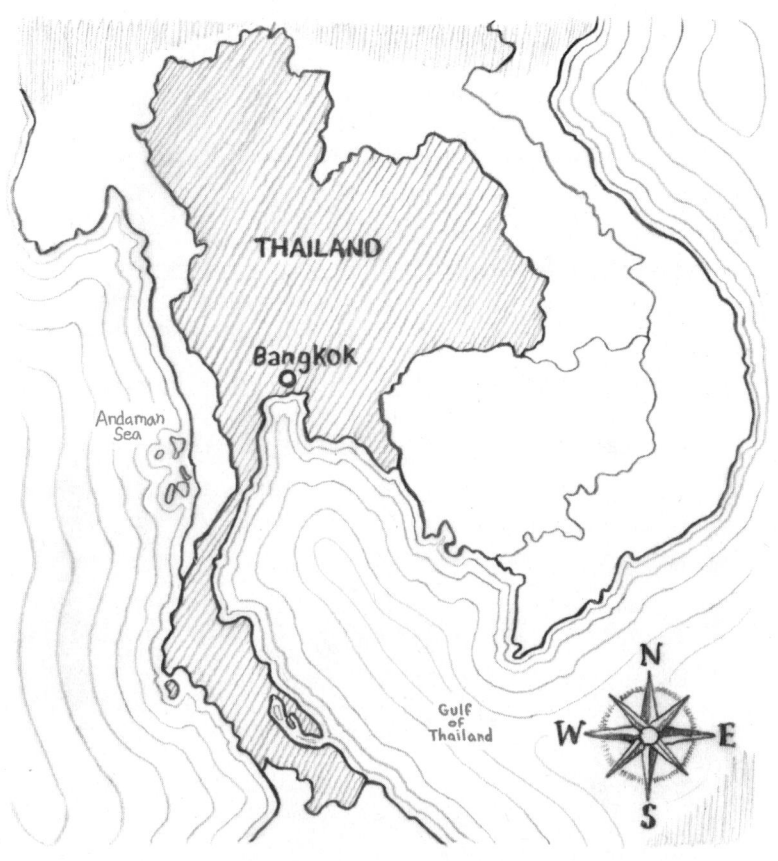

its oldest forms. Over centuries, Buddhism spread from India to many parts of Asia. According to Buddhist beliefs, all humans live in a cycle of suffering and rebirth. Once a person dies, they are reborn and start the cycle all over again.

However, people can overcome this vicious cycle by performing good deeds and letting go of negative feelings like greed and hatred. The Buddhist idea of karma says that our actions control what happens to us. By practicing good behavior and ways of thinking, people can eventually break free of the cycle of suffering and get to a state of freedom called nirvana.

Buddha statue

Songkran

Songkran is an important holiday in the Thai Buddhist tradition in addition to being a celebration of the new year. It is also known as the Water Festival and is a time for purification and renewal. As Songkran gets closer, people busy themselves with cleaning their houses, places of business, and Buddhist temples.

The first day of the festival, April 13, is considered the end of the old year. Families might wake up early and visit their local temple, bringing offerings of homemade food, fruit, and sweet treats to the monks. They pray and pour perfumed water over statues of the Buddha to wash them. Younger members of the family may also pour water over elder family members' hands as a sign of respect. These kinds of good deeds are part of making "merit." In Buddhism, people believe that merit making can help improve their next life and help them reach nirvana.

Songkran may sound like a serious holiday, but as it goes on, it becomes very lively and fun. Parades wind down the streets, sometimes featuring a woman dressed as Miss Songkran in traditional clothing. But the most festive part of the holiday is the huge water fights that break out. April is a very hot time of year in Thailand.

Because water is so important on Songkran, it has become a tradition for people to splash one another using just about anything, including buckets, hoses, water balloons, and water squirters. They are symbolically cleansing one another, cooling down, and simply having fun!

Major cities such as Bangkok see their streets

Songkran in Bangkok

turn into massive water parties. People make sure to dress in clothing that they don't mind getting wet, because when they're outside during Songkran, they know they will get soaked. Along with the water fights, the party atmosphere includes music and dancing.

The Legend of Songkran

A popular legend explains the origin of Songkran. According to the story, there once was a very wise and gifted young man named Dhammapala. A god, Kabila Mahaphrom, became jealous of this man and came down to earth. He presented Dhammapala with three riddles. If Dhammapala was not able to solve the riddles in seven days, he would lose his head. But if he did solve the riddles in that time, the god would cut off his own head instead. After thinking over the riddles, Dhammapala was becoming discouraged. But then he heard a mother eagle telling her baby the answers to the riddles. He went to the god and told him the answers, and the god cut off his own head. However, the god's head was so hot that if it fell to the earth, it would burn the land, boil away all the water, and cause a drought. So the god's seven daughters took the head to a cave in heaven to prevent this. During Songkran, one of the daughters takes the head out of the cave, washes it, and carries it in a parade that ends with a great feast. The daughter who carries the god's head on Songkran is known as Miss Songkran.

Another popular tradition during Songkran is building sand pagodas, which look similar to sandcastles. This activity may take place on a beach or at a temple. Families bring sand to temples as a way of symbolically bringing back the sand that has stuck to their feet and been carried away over the past year. Then they use the sand to build pagodas and stupas (domed shrines), that are decorated with colorful paper flags and flowers.

Sand pagoda

Contests are held for the best sand pagoda, with some pagodas becoming very detailed and soaring high into the sky. Sometimes a coin is buried in the sand pagodas, and when the festival is over, children dig into the pagodas to find the coins.

As with other new year celebrations, food is an important part of Songkran. Families may gather for a big meal with festive dishes made for the occasion. And between water fights, festivalgoers might grab snacks from street food vendors. However, there are no specific foods that are traditionally served at Songkran. Instead, Songkran foods vary from region to region and from family to family.

One household may have special dishes that they have made every Songkran for years. Curries, fried whole fish, and slow-cooked meat stews are all dishes that might show up on a Songkran table. Also popular during the festivities are cold drinks and frozen treats, since the weather is so hot.

Curry

Songkran combines religious tradition, family togetherness, and a great sense of fun into one vibrant and joyful celebration.

It is not difficult to see why it is the most important and beloved holiday of the year in Thailand.

CHAPTER 8
A Truly Global Holiday

Lunar New Year is celebrated on almost every continent and in most major cities. Large urban centers such as London, Vancouver, and Sydney all have public parades and festivals every Lunar New Year. People of many backgrounds are

Lunar New Year in London

joining in on the tradition, and so it is being recognized as an official holiday by more and more governments.

In the United States, California was the first state to declare Lunar New Year an official holiday. It did so in 2022. After San Francisco, Los Angeles holds one of the biggest Lunar New Year celebrations in the state. The festivities last for weeks there, capped off with the annual Golden Dragon Parade, with appearances by Asian American celebrities. Even Disneyland has its own official Lunar New Year celebration. There is a special parade featuring characters from the movie *Mulan*, appearances by beloved Disney characters, such as Mickey, wearing red-and-gold clothing, and themed activities and shows. Festive food honoring Lunar New Year can be found in the park, such as a mandarin orange cake shaped like a glistening orange ball and a bright violet taro-flavored Vietnamese iced coffee.

Los Angeles Golden Dragon Parade

In 2023, Colorado became the second state to recognize Lunar New Year as an official holiday. Lunar New Year festivals can be found all around the state, but Denver holds one of the largest.

Their festival lasts for two days and includes activities like dragon ice carving, lion dancing, and even K-pop dance classes.

K-pop dance class

In New York State, Governor Kathy Hochul signed a bill in 2023 officially declaring Lunar New Year a school holiday. All children in the state now get the day off from school so that they can celebrate the holiday with their families. New York City has three major Chinatowns, with one in the borough of Manhattan, one in Queens, and one in Brooklyn. Each of these locations puts on a Lunar New Year festival complete with parades, fireworks, and performances.

Lunar New Year in New York City

Major cultural institutions such as the Metropolitan Museum of Art and the New York Philharmonic also put on exhibits and performances specifically for Lunar New Year. And, of course, people crowd the restaurants of Chinatown and Koreatown to dine on Lunar New Year foods.

Because New Jersey has the fourth-largest Asian American and Pacific Islander population in the United States, Governor Phil Murphy declared Lunar New Year a public holiday in

2024. That year, the city of East Rutherford hosted the Lunar New Year Spectacular, followed the next day by the Lantern Festival Gala. The city of Newark held a day's worth of festivities, including a dragon parade, a fan dance and drum performance by students from a Korean school, and DJ music to make the celebration even more lively.

Fan dance

The city of Boston has also made Lunar New Year an official holiday. Boston's Chinatown holds a Lunar New Year festival where people can participate in activities like making Lunar New Year decorations, practicing calligraphy, and sculpting Chinese zodiac animals out of clay. There is of course a parade through Chinatown. The Museum of Fine Arts even hosts Lunar New Year activities where guests can learn Chinese brush painting, how to perform a saebae, and try on Korean hanbok.

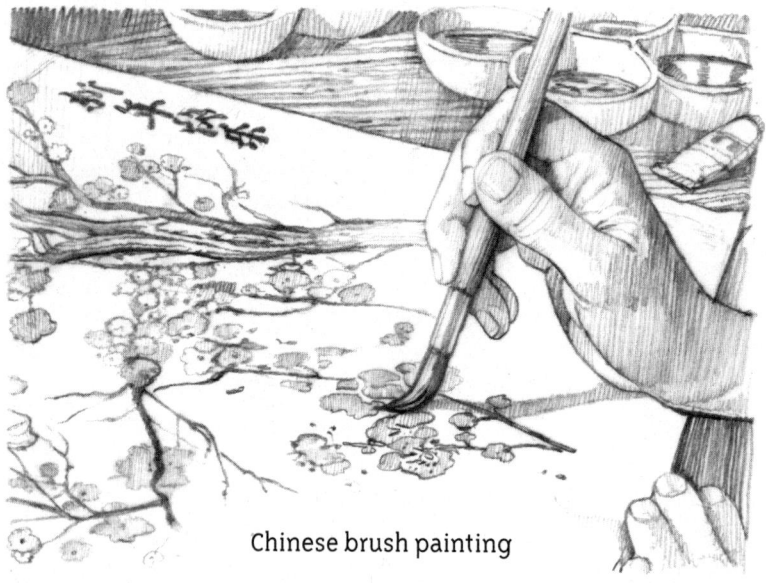

Chinese brush painting

"Feeding the lion"

Though some states and cities may not recognize Lunar New Year as an official holiday, they still hold large celebrations. In the city of Honolulu, Hawaii, there is an all-day festival. Groups of lion dancers gather in Chinatown for an event where people can "feed the lion," or put cash in red envelopes in the mouths of the lions. Doing this is thought to bring luck and ward off evil spirits. Miami also celebrates Lunar New Year. One of the most spectacular events is a lighted lantern festival, which features handcrafted silk lanterns shaped like jungle animals, sea creatures, and more. The city of Las Vegas goes all out, with many of the hotels and resorts being richly decorated with lanterns, banners, and lush flowers. Seattle holds an evening Lunar New Year market where people can stroll around enjoying artisan booths, food, and performances. The Seattle Chinese Garden also hosts a Lunar New Year lantern festival.

The spread of Lunar New Year can be seen  beyond the yearly parades and festivals. The US Postal Service began issuing Lunar New Year stamps back in 1992, and they are now some of the most popular special stamps that they offer.

LUNAR NEW YEAR
• FOREVER USA • 2024

Lego also designs Lunar New Year sets as part of their seasonal collections. These sets depict things like the Lantern Festival, dragons, and family Lunar New Year traditions. Collectible Lunar New Year Barbie dolls are released each year. The dolls wear miniature Lunar New Year outfits inspired by the traditional versions.

And because buying new clothing is symbolically important for the holiday, many clothing and handbag designers create special Lunar New Year collections featuring lucky colors and zodiac symbols.

Lunar New Year celebrations have changed over the centuries to reflect current times. At the very beginning, they were simply a way to celebrate the coming of spring and to look with hope for a good year ahead. Today, Lunar New Year is a hugely popular worldwide holiday with elaborate shows, parades, and feasts. Children might receive money through digital red envelopes rather than paper ones, and families can connect through video chat if they can't meet in person. But even during times when the celebration of Lunar New Year was more uncommon, people worked hard to keep its traditions alive. They taught these traditions to their children and shared them with friends. They followed lucky customs, retold stories, and made delicious Lunar New Year foods. Through actions both big and small—from government

proclamations to small family gatherings—
Lunar New Year has persisted as a joyful reminder
of the renewal that each new year brings.

Timeline of Lunar New Year

c. 1500–1400 BCE	The Chinese lunar-solar calendar is first used in China to plan agricultural growing seasons
1600–1046 BCE	Lunar New Year begins to be celebrated in China during the Shang dynasty
c. 700 BCE	The first records appear of the Korean Lunar New Year, Seollal
c. 206 BCE	The animals of the Chinese zodiac are established
c. 200 BCE	Fireworks are invented in China
c. 935 CE	Lunar New Year is one of nine major festivals in Korea during the Goryeo period
1912	China begins to use the Gregorian calendar for official matters
1953	The Lunar New Year festival and parade draws around one hundred thousand visitors to San Francisco's Chinatown
2015	Lunar New Year is declared a national holiday in the Philippines
2022	The state of California establishes Lunar New Year as an official holiday
2023	The state of New York declares Lunar New Year a school holiday

Timeline of the World

c. 4000 BCE	People begin to use oxen to pull plows on farms
c. 2500 BCE	The first of the great pyramids of Egypt is built
c. 1600 BCE	China begins to be ruled by dynasties
c. 500 BCE	Taoism is founded in China
	Buddhism arises in India
918 CE	The Korean Peninsula is unified into the kingdom of Goryeo
1949	The People's Republic of China is established
1969	The Apollo 11 lunar module, *Eagle*, lands on the moon
1975	The Vietnam War ends
1983	The internet is invented
1990	The Hubble Space Telescope is launched into orbit
2007	The first Apple iPhone goes on sale
2022	Beijing hosts the Winter Olympics, becoming the first city to host both the Summer and Winter Olympics

Bibliography

*Books for young readers

Baclig, Cristina Eloisa. "What to Know About Lunar New Year Celebrations in PH." *Philippine Daily Inquirer*, February 6, 2024. https://newsinfo.inquirer.net/1900113/what-to-know-about-lunar-new-year-celebrations-in-ph.

Bodde, Derk. *Festivals in Classical China: New Year and Other Annual Observances During the Han Dynasty, 206 B.C.– A.D. 220.* Princeton: Princeton University Press, 1975.

"Chinatown Din Hails Year of the Serpent." *San Francisco Examiner*, February 14, 1953.

"Chinese New Year Fete Goes On." *San Francisco Examiner*, February 15, 1953.

*Cho, Tina. *Korean Celebrations: Festivals, Holidays and Traditions.* North Clarendon, VT: Tuttle Publishing, 2019.

Crump, William D. *Encyclopedia of New Year's Holidays Worldwide.* Jefferson, NC: McFarland & Company, Inc., Publishers, 2008.

Davidson, Rose. "Songkran." *National Geographic Kids.* https://kids.nationalgeographic.com/celebrations/article/songkran.

France-Presse, Agence. "Why Vietnam Is Celebrating the Year of the Cat, Not the Rabbit." *Voice of America.* January 21, 2023. https://www.voanews.com/a/why-vietnam-is-celebrating-the-year-of-the-cat-not-the-rabbit/6928201.html#.

"Happy New Year—With a Splash of Cool Water!" *Asian and African Studies Blog*. British Library, April 13, 2015. https://blogs.bl.uk/asian-and-african/2015/04/happy-new-year-with-a-splash-of-cool-water-.html.

Hegarty, Siobhan. "Celebrate: Songkran." *SBS Food*. Updated March 30, 2021. https://www.sbs.com.au/food/article/celebrate-songkran/3u1ja8q58.

Hu, William C. *Chinese New Year: Fact and Folklore*. Ann Arbor, MI: Ars Ceramica, 1991.

Kaur, Harmeet. "How Asian Americans Are Keeping Lunar New Year Traditions Alive." CNN, January 19, 2023. https://www.cnn.com/2023/01/19/us/asian-americans-lunar-new-year-traditions-cec/.

Laing, Jennifer, and Warwick Frost, eds. *Rituals and Traditional Events in the Modern World*. New York: Routledge, 2015.

*Lee, Jen Sookfong. *Chinese New Year: A Celebration for Everyone*. Victoria, BC: Orca Book Publishers, 2017.

"Lunar New Year Around Asia." *Asia Society*. https://asiasociety.org/philippines/lunar-new-year-around-asia.

Na, Kyung Soo, ed. *Encyclopedia of Korean Seasonal Customs*. Seoul: National Folk Museum of Korea, 2010.

Ngoc, Huu, and Barbara Cohen. *Tet: The Vietnamese Lunar New Year*. Hanoi: Thê Giói Publishers, 1997.

Nowakowski, Teresa. "South Koreans Just Got Younger, Thanks to a New Law." *Smithsonian Magazine*, June 30, 2023. https://www.smithsonianmag.com/smart-news/south-korea-international-age-180982458/.

"100,000 Help Usher in New Year at Chinatown." *San Francisco Examiner*, February 16, 1953.

"100,000 Launch Year of Serpent." *Oakland Tribune*, February 16, 1953.

*Otto, Carolyn. *Celebrate Chinese New Year*. Washington, DC: National Geographic, 2009.

Romulo, Liana. *Filipino Celebrations: A Treasure of Feasts and Festivals*. North Clarendon, VT: Tuttle Publishing, 2011.

Sarnoff, Leah. "Lunar New Year 2024: Which US Cities and States Recognize It as a Public Holiday." ABC News, February 8, 2024. https://abcnews.go.com/US/lunar-new-year-2024-us-cities-states-recognize/story?id=106799053.

Wong, Wesley R., with Catherine Lenox. *Mr. Chinatown: The Legacy of H. K. Wong*. Duvall, WA: Write Contact, LLC, 2021.

Yen, Chiou-ling. *Making an American Festival: Chinese New Year in San Francisco's Chinatown*. Berkeley: University of California Press, 2008.

Yuan, Haiwang. "The Origin of Chinese New Year." *Western Kentucky University TopSCHOLAR*. https://digitalcommons.wku.edu/dlps_fac_pub/115.

Website

Encyclopedia of Korean Culture: encykorea.aks.ac.kr

San Francisco's Lunar New Year parade, 2024

A Chūn Jié celebration in China in the early twentieth century

A marching band performs for Lunar New Year in New York City, 1960.

A family celebrates Chūn Jié with a special dinner in China, 1999.

Two dancers perform during a Lunar New Year parade in London, 2024.

Two performers wear traditional costumes during a Songkran celebration in Thailand, 1998.

Korean teenagers jump on a seesaw, part of Seollal celebrations, in 1954.

An artist in Vancouver, Canada, sells special artwork for the
Year of the Snake, 2025.

Drummers perform at a Lunar New Year celebration
in Denver, Colorado, 2024.

Lion dancers perform at the London Lunar New Year celebration, 2025.

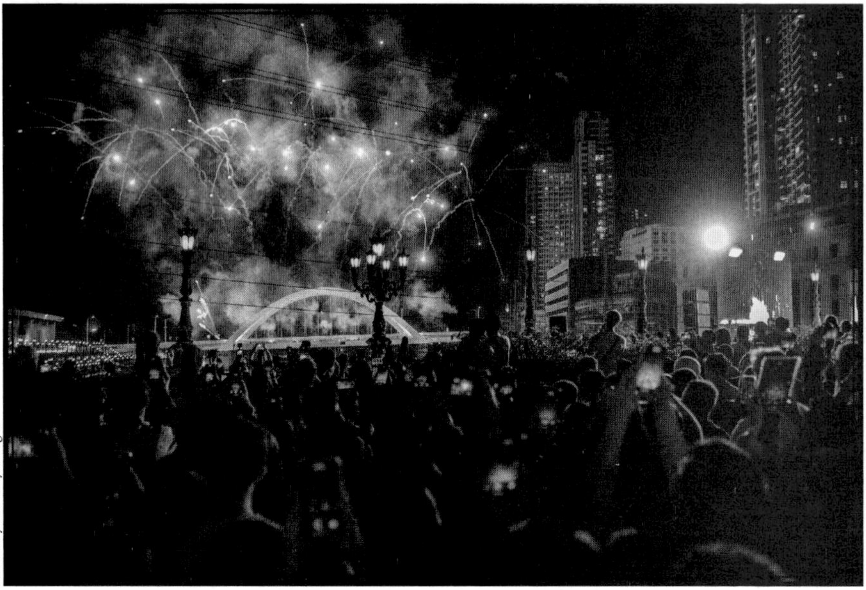

Ezra Acayan/Getty Images

Filipinos celebrate Lunar New Year with fireworks in Binondo, the Chinatown of Manila, 2025.

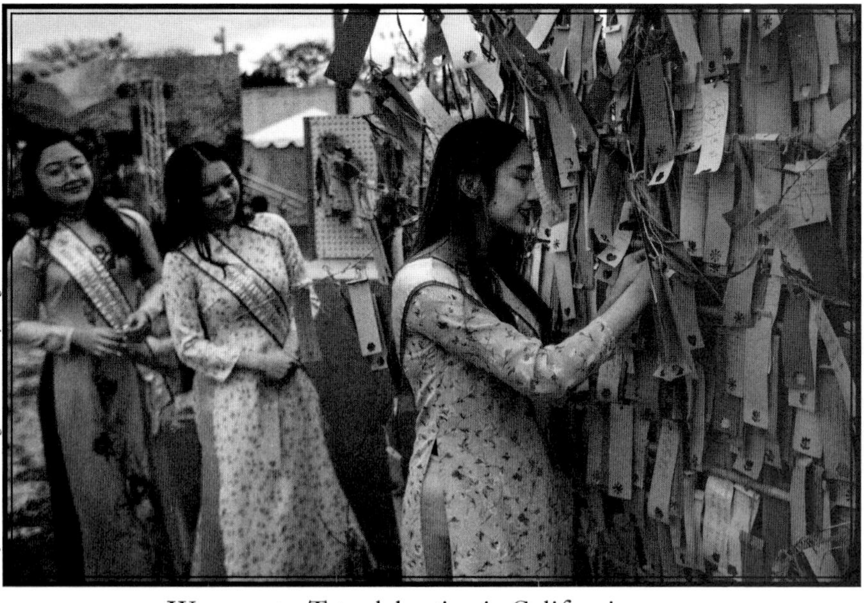

Allen J. Schaben/Los Angeles Times/Getty Images

Women at a Tet celebration in California, 2023

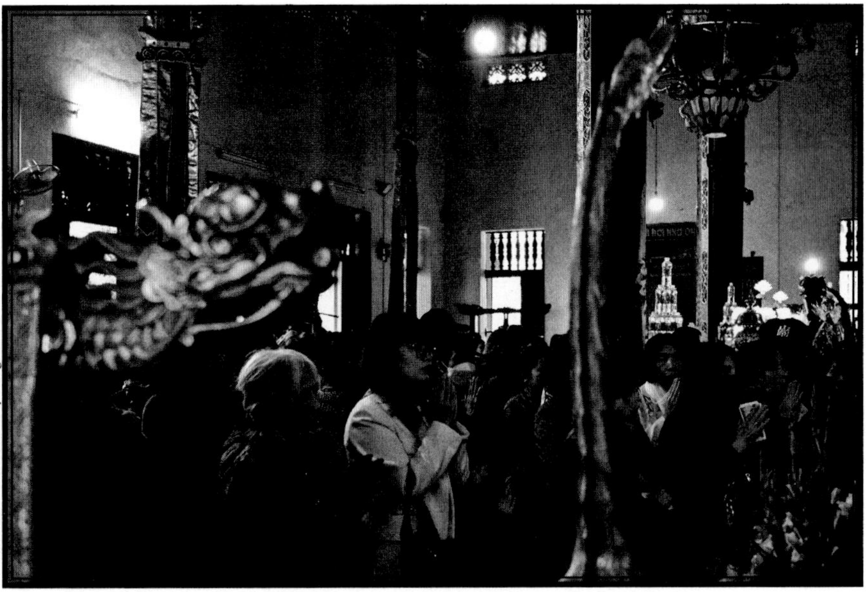

NHAC NGUYEN/AFP/Getty Images

Vietnamese people pray during a Tet celebration, 2025.

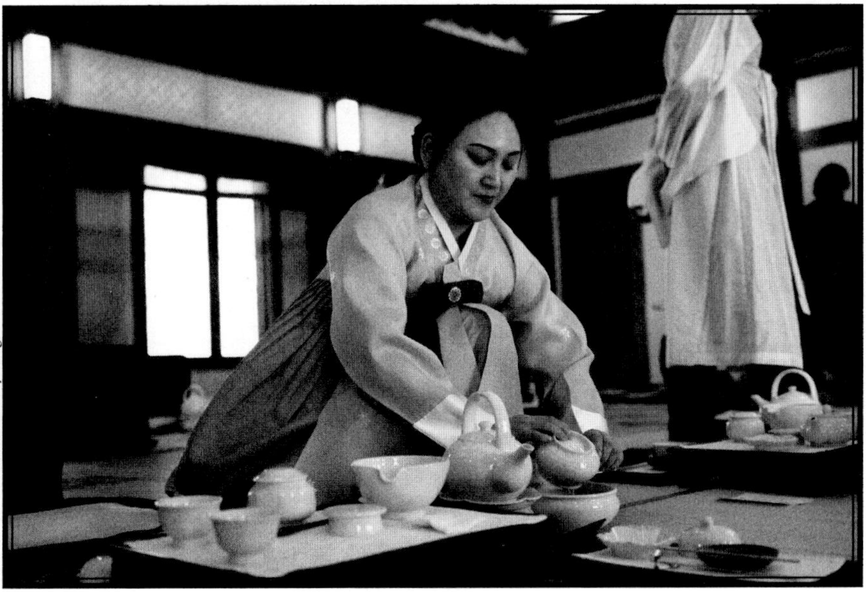

Hwawon Ceci Lee/Anadolu/Getty Images

A Korean woman wearing a hanbok participates in a tea ceremony during Seollal, 2025.

A Chūn Jié drone show in China, 2025

Two children splash each other with water during Songkran in Thailand.